Mrs. I

I am honored to have gotten to know your child Chynna. They are a kind and compassionate human being who brings joy to all who surround them. I hope you are proud as a mother for raising such a quality person, and I hope this book gives you the tiniest fraction of joy that your child does everyday.

Peace, love, and all the Best,

E. C.

The Final Light

A Collection of Poems to the Glory of Life

E. Christine

All rights reserved. No part of this book shall be reproduced or transmitted in any form or by any means, electronic, mechanical, magnetic, photographic including photocopying, recording or by any information storage and retrieval system, without prior written permission of the publisher. No patent liability is assumed with respect to the use of the information contained herein. Although every precaution has been taken in the preparation of this book, the publisher and author assume no responsibility for errors or omissions. Neither is any liability assumed for damages resulting from the use of the information contained herein.

Copyright © 2016 by Elisabeth Christine Woldeyohannes

ISBN 978-1-4958-1142-5
ISBN 978-1-4958-1143-2 eBook
Library of Congress Control Number: 2016915505

This is a work of fiction. Names, characters, places, and incidents either are the product of the author's imagination or are used fictitiously. Any resemblance to actual events or locales or persons, living or dead, is entirely coincidental.

Published August 2016

INFINITY PUBLISHING
1094 New DeHaven Street, Suite 100
West Conshohocken, PA 19428-2713
Toll-free (877) BUY BOOK
Local Phone (610) 941-9999
Fax (610) 941-9959
Info@buybooksontheweb.com
www.buybooksontheweb.com

"Thus, great with child to speak, and helpless in my throes,

Biting my truant pen, beating myself for spite—

'Fool,' said my Muse to me, 'look in thy heart and write.'"

Sir Phillip Sidney, *Astrophil and Stella*

I would like to give my warmest thanks to each and every soul who has kissed my life in such a way to inspire or nurture the words within this book. I give my entire heart and gratitude to my parents, Dr. Mentesinot Woldeyohannes and Kirsten Clements, my loving family, my mentors and editors, Dr. Gary Wiener, Sarah Nazarian, Professor Randy Schiff, and my mother—without whom this could not be possible—and each and every sunflower of a friend or beautiful momentary light that touched me to music in my soul.

I give my thanks to the trees and the Earth,
to the moon and the stars,
to the thought of dreams and galaxies blinking and fading away just to be rediscovered in brilliance by the vision of a new eye.
And to you, Euterpe's voice in human form:
As much as the sea requires shore to beat its cares against,

Every writer needs a muse.

The Final Light

Table of Contents

Dawn 1

Day 17

Dusk 25

Dark 47

Sensus 75

Dawn.

To Wonder of Lilies and Stars

To wonder of her wondering
at the sight of mountain caps
and fields of lavender
with lilies in her hair.

And to picture her hand leading before mine
as soft and fair and enveloping
as star-kissed sea-foam lapping
at the edges of man.

To dream of her dreaming,
little feet kicking under covers
pulled too tight
with the sensation of flight.

And to imagine her tongue
pressed against grinning teeth,
clicking to garden snakes as
serpents of dungeons
and dispelling flies as gate-keeping dragons.

To gaze upon her startled lights
glittering with mirrors of stars—
and to watch a warrior weep
with child's heart—and bend—
and begin to grow again.

Messengers

Every parted, purple cloud
answers my contorted, crooked brow.
With a sullen shrug I turn away;
they lay dormant one more day.

Knowing, they knock just one more time—
watching, waiting, their kind eyes patient,
they whisper niceties through the door,
the kind I hadn't bargained for.

Yet again I feel unworthy,
snatch my sullen carcass from the door,
and I bury my head in my sleeve,
there is no escape nor reprieve.

The cyan sky does not lose
the faith it has justly found in me.
The messengers never turn an eye;
they refuse to bid goodbye.

And thus they wait, back toward the door,
for me to come and bid them welcome:
they do not press nor force their entrance;
they sit mum as if in penance.

A creak, a crack, the door does breathe
open as my friend does speak hello;
I greet the presence with open arm,
and to myself I do no harm.

The sky, enlightened, opens
and, when I am ready, takes my hand—
breaking the cycle of callous pain,
thus prepared to live again.

THANKFUL

The grass beneath my feet,
the Earth beneath my toes,
wind-swept hair that's star-kissed sweet
and moonlight on my nose.

The touch of gentle hands,
the precious hearts that hold—
I'll never find time in sands
for I shall not grow old.

And every piece of sky
holds something vast and new—
a thousand worlds blink and fly
up in the black and blue.

The friends I meet and love,
forever in no time,
memories in thoughts above,
forever in my prime.

The grass beneath my feet,
the Earth beneath my toes,
every day the goodness meets
a peace that no one knows.

THE ABYSS OF MORNING

When I tell you I'm breathing, I don't know what for;
the lines in my heart drape the open floor.
To see a piece of my lung, a slab of dark soot:
the cancer, the mind, in dark lies stay put.
A Dragon's flame, a white trail, brushes tortured tongue—
leaves holes in my soul where innocence once hung.
Tip-toe, do not wake me, my own mind is afraid
of what promises shall break and what lies remade.
An organ of addiction, a seed in my breast,
must sleep the eternal so that I may rest.
Hark— the seed brings new breath to a forest of dead,
what consumes gives life to words far ahead.

Dawn

I revel in how night never comes in winter:
there is no descending, no dusk, no dark.
I turn my eyes toward the forest dear
and become lost in her joyful song.

Instead of blackness, a thousand tiny eyes:
a thousand tiny beads of sand
on which starlight glistens
and extends to reach my hand.

It may be Spring that bears the most fruit,
that overpowers the death and decay,
but is it not better to coexist forever
as warm colors amongst the gray?

There may be that dissipation of glory,
of an epic, uplifting song,
but I know in my heart that the best thing of all
is the eternal expression of dawn.

The Cycle of Life

I live for the beady eyes in the catfelt—
A glistle here, a glistle there,
gliding across the rushes with a shiver and a shake.
Screeches rise up from the thicket;
mothers cry to sons and sons cry to captains,
clutching their breasts that beat
to the glory and the pain of war.
They veer and ascend, lacking now
the twin harmony of freshly-painted wings,
substituting instead the madness
of crimson-spattered uniforms and panicked eyes
that entwine far into the deep, marigold sky.
The beady eyes in the catfelt sparkle with a ravenous need,
poised above the weak and the meek
and those too broken and fatigued to rise.
But behind, oh behind
the beady eyes that elude the rushes wild
and flirt with the moon on the glint of the lake,
another pair, too, awaits.

Elapse

Up comes the day, down descends the night;
morning dawns as mourning wakes at holy morning light.
Well promises kept good, in the safety of the keep,
and I had traveled miles
before I began to sleep.

Ireland

With voice soft and eyes closed
and lips soft as pearly gates;
smile broad and cheeks rose
and grins passing nose to nose;

Fingers intertwined
and eyes icy comets blue,
voices caught and decision resigned,
myself I seek; me I find,
infinity within a few.

With hearts in tandem,
energy aligned,
let me pass from me to you.

WHAT LOVE CAN DO

If you really loved me,
I would embrace your arms as the sweet caress of the open sea,
and your hands of seaweed would weave around to buoy me.
If you really loved me,
never again would I fight the tumult of feverish aching sleep,
for your hands of linen would wrap around to comfort me.
If you really loved me,
colors would appear the constructs of unruly dreams,
and your rays of sunshine would breathe a new life into me.

Fidem in Spe Habeo

I have faith in hope
and the power it holds.

I have faith that in all
the everlasting concavities
there will be a glimpse of the twinkling cosmos—

that spritely stars will parade
in vibrant arrays,
skirts of galaxies perpetually spiraling
into the deep, dark, beyond.

There will always be hands
of glittering silver
to pull you back from the blackness.

HUMMINGBIRD

What flutter could these sweet little wings be?
Darting and dashing through the plains of open air,
iridescent and sparkling against the midsummer sun.
She peeps hello and bows away,
fleeting and falling and tumbling and crashing
through currents and waves of peaceful breeze,
enlightened and humming amidst the midsummer air.

Calm your jitters, you sweet little thing;
cease your trembling and urgency—
little wings should not beat against your breast to hover
when they may teach you how to soar.

Alas, your presence is welcome, you sweet little thing—
A place set with coffee and crackers
before these walls are filled with banging, booming—
peaceful in the light of midsummer dawn.

KISS THE GIRL

And at the end of all things,
I mean this in the kindest way,
I hope you meet someone from
whose eyes you'll never sway.

And I hope she's good to you,
fills you with courage to be strong,
and I hope that by her side
rough times are never long.

I hope that she's worth risking
all your future and what you know,
and when this girl takes your lips
you let your feelings show.

I know I cannot be her,
and that is honestly okay—
You deserve that lovely girl,
please marry her someday.

This is What I Live For:

Buildings capped in light ushering the clouds into the sky,
trails of smoke that eddy out into the blue, orange, and white,
the sound of sweet guitar carried by joyful breezes to
	my window,
the sun kissing the trees that play along their winding shadows,
the girl surrounded by daises drenched in heaven's
	sweet embrace,
and the knowledge that I'll have it all again the next
	time I awake.

DAY.

INVENTION

Eyes light the stars above the great beyond—
looking glass to eternal blissful moors
that dance to the flames of your heart's own fire.
How it moves my soul to quiver and shake
to stand as witness to your breathing mind,
cascading down to break Oceanus,
whose waves threaten man with limitations.
That imposing sea, scourge to invention,
does not carry the might of Juno's hand
to break your mast and send your sails away.
Instead there stands Eve with arms extended,
and there, take a bite from her radiance.
How it moves me to music in my soul
to stand as witness to your lovely muse,
who, hidden, tumbles out and gives away
the divinity behind the motor
which turns and designs glory with your hands.
And there lies the heaven in man's delight.

Pick Your Poison

I smell Gin now whenever I breathe,
and I can see blue in glass
and lemons upon lemons floating in morphine.
I can feel your skin when you are not here,
and I can kiss the breeze and taste you,
and now I love Gin.

Cloudy Mornings

There's a time for thunderstorms;
where we can feels the ghosts of raindrops past
and we can reflect on summer's dawn and summer's end,
as leaves breathe and brush against the dewy grass
and feel their hearts beat again.

There's a time for tears and heartaches,
but, Lord, let mine be for joy.
There's a time for pain and sorrow,
but, Lord let my rain be warm—
there's a time for missing you,
but, Lord, let you come home.

Lord, let me know,
I swear, let me know,
and let little feet dance in little brown puddles;
let them not suffer in constricting little shoes.

God, there will be a time for night,
but, Lord, allow stars to turn the dark to day—
and let me bask in their light.

SPIRITS

How our earthly vessels elope matters not,
for soon our fleeting realm shall forever be forgot,
and peaks as flimsy as the turn of our beliefs
still shall not crumble at the visage of our griefs.

How our souls survive the scourge matters all the more,
for there we shall pass beyond our mortal door.
By which way I was loved, by many or by none,
will fade from remembrance when our story has been done.

May how I grasped each breath be the only matter to me;
may I not hold back, take care, or scramble for the "we",
for our options are wide as our open, passing moor:
bright and inviting, each never known before.

TEXTING

How much can a text contain?
Can the feverish swell of her fingers press boldness into the letters?
Can her wanting lip curled and captured
beneath unaware teeth convey itself through waves of air?
Alas, may you, one on the other side of sphere,
know the way her fingers tremble in the subjected cold,
know with what urgency she shields her thumbs from the rain
to pass her message through the shifting breeze?
May you be sitting there silent, waiting,
with lip curled under unapologetic teeth,
fingers tapping feverishly through the stagnant air,
hands bare to face the subjected cold.

Deliverance

From the forest to the sea
and mountains high and in-between,
the path I walk is laid before
my sodden shoes upon the shore.

Let them not halt to bending root;
let them find a quiet, quivering nook
where they can rest their weary score
upon the sand upon the shore.

And let me leave my baggage there,
in the hot fatigue of summer air,
and let my soul unburdened soar
to a whisper far beyond the shore.

For there is not a place that seems
better than in the arms of he
who holds my form above the floor,
who bears my body from the shore.

Yes, not a place, it seems to me,
better than in the arms of he
who seeks to give me so much more
than I would find out on the shore.

YOUNG LOVE

She was the night sky,
glistening with divine wonder
and playful mystery,
laced with a wise patience.

There she danced her dance
with the sun at her side,
leaning over her as a cosmic protectorate.
At the same time she moves to move him
and eclipses his day.

He was the light-lit morn,
beaming down with pristine joy—
an undying happiness
intertwined with a regal knowing.

There he danced his dance
with the moon at his side,
rising up to steal his cosmic control.
At the same time he grips her in embrace
and captures her orbit.

There they danced a cosmic dance
with man as witness,
with young eyes embarrassed to be caught
against the brick wall.

Dusk.

Wyrd

Perhaps one day we shall gaze upon moonless sky,
the same compelling that betwixt my heart and yours,
and thus condemned our souls, both young and old, to die,
and barren Love's fields be with pleasure lacking chores.

So I turn my misery to a Force on high;
reason we may find behind golden iron doors.
And yet we may in mockery be seized, and sigh,
deceived to come upon the Styx's most wicked shores.

Bound by coffin black we may find our trembling care,
whether placed by the fires of hell or heaven's light.
The path before our feet reads "travel, if ye dare" –
only in courage our timid love be requite.

Pray our metal pure, and falsehood claim not our day,
for your arms be delight, if tricky powers may.

THE ASTRONAUT

When I was young I'd sit and reach for a star
thousands and thousands of miles in the deep, dark sky.
My mother would come out and sit with me
and say that I could snatch it— I need only to try.
So I'd lean on the clean-cut grass for the speck of white
in the deep, dark blue and cry
when I fell back down to Earth;
The twinkling trickster hardly let out a sigh.
Soon I realized, the speck was a place I could not reach,
and my mother's words were laced with lie—
I settled for faded brick walls and narrow, crowded halls
and let the spirits of my jumping child die.
Imperatives of "dream" turned to "be realistic,"
and knowledge from what I could find to what I could buy.
But one day, I lay out in that dewy green grass,
looking up at that orb in the deep, dark sky,
and I knew that if I stuck out my hand and reached,
I'd have it—
I need only to learn how to fly.

Giving Away Your Daughter

Let the little girl kiss your toes goodnight,
and let her begin each day by basking in your light.
Let her giggly reign, bright forevermore,
illuminate scattered subjects strewn across the floor.

And let her ride upon your feet to breakfast down below,
and pray you never let a solemn sadness show.
May she embrace fluffy creatures and not know any pain
and meet more subjects among the grass so she can
    further reign.

Doubt not the strength that fair palm loves to send—
let you guide her hand along up to an arrow's end.
And when it is time, you let that hand go;
watch her kiss the tear-drop eyes of freshly laden snow.

And when she descends down stairs, let you find a
    woman there—
may you let no feeling slip but love from your stare.
For she is like your muse, a brilliance you've never seen—
Ah, she is not your princess, for she has always been a queen.

GAME OVER

Fire, fire
eyes of rolling waves to break the flame,
crisp outer edges,
fire.
Hesitation, pressure, hovering above and burning
within.
Frozen, the flames break apart,
time stands still:
darting gazing, piercing knowing,
the sweetest softness on your brow—
Still water,
cheeks together,
eyes barely apart—
game over.

Time

Time, time, time—
the clock ticks its endless pressure,
and pressure too forms along my skull.
If there be no time to love,
no time to caress the gentle fronds of the growing things
that guide the entrance to spring,
then time does not exist at all.
It is imaginary, arbitrary,
confined to plastics and dusty mechanisms,
confined to our winding keys and our straight-laced lives.
Time is held eternal in glints of sunlight on the water's edge,
yet it escapes in breaths taken too quickly,
too suddenly,
as the seconds pass to open air.
We create our own time,
without us, its power shakes and quakes
under foundations of dust and repetition.
If there be no time for what time was meant to be,
then it means not a thing at all.

Tracing the Blue

5:30 felt like drowning—
the ocean kissed fall,
looked back on the past,
and sighed.

5:00 was dark before—
demons stalked me,
red in a looming shadow,
and grinned.

4:28 felt so late—
the blue consumed day,
time, running, glanced behind
and hid.

This ocean was once the shelter of my solitude,
but now I'm sending peace out through the blue—
It's 6:44,
and I feel so close to you.

Irrational Lover

I am an irrational lover.
Instead of a rose, I'll give you a lotus flower
and show you just where our love can grow:
Embers reside in meteorites
and the flint in hearts of stars.
Time shall lose all meaning:
Ten years from now the world is mine,
in hundreds, the effort's fleeting.
Your breath will be my breath;
your laughter, my laughter.
I will tell my friends about the little looks you give me,
the crook of a smile that awakens when no one else can see.
While I am rejoicing in our fire,
kindling our flame,
I will discover
that you hardly think of me at all.

YOU

I want you.
The undeniable you.
Everything that encompasses you.
Your breath, your scent, your laughter, your rage,
every memory of childhood that has now begun to fade.
I want you,
the unapologetic you.
The you that hides in the dark corners of your mind
and approaches only to sniff the hand extended.
I want that you to want me.

VERITAS

If you do not love me,
let me know—

Do not kiss my back softly
and pull my head close to your chest.

If you do not love me,
make it clear—

Do not show me the things
that send your soul to flight.

But if you love me, by God,
show my heart;

Convince my broken mind that
there is more behind that spark.

Take your walls apart
and turn the stone to dust;

Let me be your queen,
and more than just your lust.

I See Your Good in Everything

You solemn, cloudy, dust-like morn,
why do you still make me believe in love?
Hope clawing at fetters, stifled by disgrace—
you'd think this dark should be enough.

Even drops of saddened, slow-paced rain
can't tarnish the trimming of your visage.
I pull up my hood to shield my reddened ears,
and your warmth fills joy's ghostly image.

Kiss me like the running rivers
beneath the constructs of man—
The wild rushing between and
among pillars of concrete
that would push against my teeth
and run away from us in swarms of butterflies.

Hold me like our fleeting love
is everlasting amongst the stars—
Bid your column arms stand guard
to quell the threats of thundering sky
that would seek to steal the peace of heart
that in memory yet resides.

The Sege of Troye

I know a Hector of Troy,
and as he looks at me his gaze passes
past my skin to the Greeks at the wall.
Give me not the love of Paris, who kisses
my feet, who leaves the battle
to cower in my chamber.
Let me love my Hector
and stand at the wall.

Let me stand at the side of Pallas Minerva
under the thundering skies;
let the twins of Sun and Moon
put their bows abreast with my billowing fury.
Let me plead for my Hector to stay,
but let his breastplate glisten with Ares' glory—
Let him kiss the forehead of our son and mine;
let him march to die.
Let him be unafraid of what lies ahead;
let him know his valor, his *kleos*, his light—
let his bronze skin sweat and bleed
for something larger than himself.

Let him love me through his honor;
let me know him through his duty;
let me kiss my Hector goodbye with pride—
let me not gaze upon a coward
trembling behind those brave, blue eyes.

Let me be a queen to a worthy hero of Troy:
May the gods move to make the slaughter cease;
May Jove protect my Hector from the onset of the siege.

RED LEAVES

Alas! Be these bits of my heart
that fall crimson to the Earth,
bloodied by the sun
who turned her rays afar?
You believe it all a display,
a false show, gawking
for the attention of your gaze.
But O Glorious Light,
if only you knew: falling for them
means the end of one's life

SAY IT'S FOR YOU

Don't you understand?
Your heart is the only one left to break—
you have broken mine a thousand times,
and in breaking, my strength remake.

It is difficult indeed to end a day within a day,
but you need neither stop nor fret nor make your peace;
let the years stretch across open bleeding minutes, for me,
don't you understand?

Every second of your absence,
crumpled bits of paper,
sheets that haven't met with
sleeping shoulders since long ago—

Stop trying to save my heart,
and I'll quit scrambling for time.

Child's Play

This is what I tell myself
when my heart is blackened by unjust rage:

Each second is worth it,
sweet child in my chest,
who beats her tiny fists against terrace doors,
broken-hearted palms flattened
in defeat against windows,
watching and lamenting to courtly birds
that whisper and giggle amongst
fans of tapestry wings.
You may see them not but in bliss,
in blushes and cooing,
in songs belted from canopy castles
for all to know, even Heaven's light.
Each second you sit with that fire in your chest,
festering a loathing for your very self,
gazing upon your fine-feathered friend
beyond your grasp, is worth it.
Love cannot exist with lock and key,
my sweet child—
the sort of little girl who squeezes kittens too tightly
and will not release rabbits from her embrace.
See not yourself at fault
for bird's banging head on prison bars;
what you believed a cathedral of glory
turned into his dungeon walls.
Now, sweet child—
he does not despise you.

The Final Light

There he is, looking behind to your nose pressed 'gainst the glass,
lips and forehead smooshed,
exasperated,
and your breath,
the steam of your weeping has clouded it
(but I believe that is a smile back).
You will never be his captor,
but his release,
and, if you let it,
each second will continue to exist,
and carry on in wondrous grace.
Shun not the light of day
now that you have but the moon to see him by.

To Love Lanval

Let us run away to a castle in the sky,
spires piercing the blue as the desire in your eyes,
but do not breathe a word of our love.

If you do, I shall disappear—
my dress of tapered silk that hangs from my breast
you shall never see again.

Let my ladies always accompany us,
until we, safe in my fleeting fabric chambers,
may hold each other with no concept of time.

Oh, my Lanval, my knight,
I wish so dearly for you to run away to Avalon
and live with me in glory bright.

But, alas, you may not reveal
a single token of love to you, a single praise;
you must sit and wonder if it truly exists.

Know it in your heart, sir knight,
that our love could conquer any kingdom,
but you must settle for a world within your mind.

Once you exhale us into this realm
my legs draped over my steed's side will leave your sight,
and my procession will vanish over the horizon.

***

The Final Light

Why did you not heed my plea?
All I desired was to convince you of my reality,
to hold you in the bustling forests and sigh.

I left you with your knees in the sand,
gazing down the path you begged with all your heart
for me to gallantly strut upon.

I am not your savior, Lanval,
I begged you with my eyes and you betrayed me.
I am not of your world; you wanted more than I could give.

And now you sit and pray,
tears welling up with the bile in your throat
for me to come and release you from Arthur's hand.

You again turn towards the crowns of trees
that gracefully bend to shield the leaf-laden way,
and hope I love you more than my circumstance.

We shall see, my dear knight—
there is time yet still.

Free Fall

It was too late for me.
The barriers around my inhibitions
were torn down by rebels of love,
boots muddied and faces pale
and contorted with exasperation,
ropes tethered to bring down
the skin membrane of my chest.
You saw a grand expanse of unknown land,
littered with patches of shadow
and blinding illuminated brilliance
(and never sure which of the two was more terrifying),
and darted down the mountain side—
A whole climb rolling backwards,
the rewinding of every video we had,
all the progression of God's grace up the cliff face,
now whizzing past,
unbeknownst to your sideways glance.
You tried to pull me back—
you extended your hands on the peak
to bring me toward the borders of man.

But I cut my own tether.
I cut it long ago.
I had climbed the whole rocky pass in faith.
My feet, bare, danced across the treacherous edges,
bleeding and blistered with smiling toes—

I spread my arms and closed my eyes
with faith in the fall,
faith in the currents of wind flying past my reddened ears,
faith in my survival beyond my broken body on the forest floor.
I even had faith that you, too, perhaps,
would see my trust and be tempted to fly.
There was no going back,
it has always been too late for me.

Companions

Oh, aren't they sweet?
From afar I know that their voices are hushed and laughs hearty—
their shoulders are pressed into a single form
overlooking a single steady painting of water,
woven from sweet lines of thread,
the needle head from Cupid's own bow.
The sunlight touches them no longer:
it has left the illumination of their toes
and traverses ahead,
dissolving into the warmth of orange
that still graces the silent trees.
Oh, one turns now,
and the movement has stirred the leaves to move,
the wind to giggle and soar,
the paint on canvas to drip and run
in time with waving hands and legs curled into side—
Now one stands.
Oh, she captures this moment.
I wonder how her painting looks,
with her subject in perfect joy,
face in lunar eclipse,
lit by the visage of her dear companion…
a painting in a painting in a painting…

Dark.

Loki's Fate

I lay here and there's a pressure in my chest
as fierce as writhing snakes,
building up and coiling around my throat
to force my only air back into my lungs.
I am defined by knuckles turning pale white
as they grip incomprehensible hopes and give out,
pins and needles tingling in the ripping tissue,
sinews tearing and releasing my grasp.
I fall back down to earth.
My body is rooted in its station,
pinned by the intestines of my brood
pulled too tightly across my feeble chest;
my comfortable warmth disrupted
by the dripping of venom corroding my heart.
Odin, release me,
be kind,
do not take the children of my soul,
the lights of my day,
the glittering of sun that rises and sighs
an inconceivable glory that filters through
the bronze-covered trees,
and turn them to darkness
to consume me.
My only salvation turned to sick torment,
dripping into my heart,
as my heavy knees weaken and sink into the fabric,
as my sweat gathers in dew upon my filmy skin
to celebrate the new day,
and I begin to choke on the flowers
that I laid in my soul for you.

STUCK

There is little to do,
what, with the pit-pattering
of little feet down crooked steps
and the breeze of fair weather
kissing me at my window.
The chime of hollow voices echoes
past stalagmites of T-Shirts
still dripping with fear and mother's perfume.
What else is there besides
the poetry in my soul?
Beyond the melodious rise of my turbulent chest
with each shallow breath,
beyond the pangs in my ribcage
that reek with confusion, rank
with the fear of an undying loneliness
that comes to kiss my window.

Paper and Ink

My fragile bones threaten to fail,
cracked beams held together by no more
than paper and string—
The mosaic of my mind too many words
all smashed into one.
They extend in thin lines across the paper of my skin,
but what is a poem but paper and string?
Ink weeps its heartbreak into sunken pores,
the faint indent of the pen gallops and glides,
grasping each letter together with feeble, sweaty palms.
But together, a current runs through those arms,
the sweat turns to the musk of age,
rising from the yellowed pages to ascend my nose
and come alive before my eyes.
The ink dotes upon my yearning lips:
It is sustenance to taste,
a lover's soft fingertips to touch,
the sixth sense that is felt in the tension
that hangs in the air.
Upon that tension-ridden tip of the pen, man teeters still,
our veins traced by that living, breathing ink
that can move mountains and trace the stars
with no more than a whisper on the wind.
There we stand, wondering the fate of a fall,
senses quivering, awaiting our chance
to no longer be mosaics, but frescos,
and to form someone else
with paper and string.

The Aftertaste of Dust

What cold taste on a placid tongue
leads to fear and dread?
What has bitter ice ever sung
locked within your head?
A wave of gold, oh lovely Sif,
valor do you spark;
the taste is vain if ever spoke
'fore he makes his mark.
There's hissing fear behind his eyes
striking soldier still;
the greatest toils of his career
never lend him fill.
The smoke is clear, the tongue is numb,
rubble in the way:
here soot falls from sunken stairs;
boys begin to pray.
I know their hearts will never mend,
gauze is never done,
perhaps the warmth shall heal their souls
born from rising sun.

Doorways

The Sparrow perched upon the mast,
my mind devoid of first and last.
Janus turns his weary head East,
perhaps for silencing my beast;
all will be well.

Dark covers the old coven door,
and Satan beats his drum once more.
Pray a call of the social kind,
no more pain for my feeble mind—
I cannot feel.

In shadow we hallow this ground;
the Sparrow knows our sickened sound.
Fly out over the open sea
and see what time has done to me;
the door is closed.

I cannot think to run my eyes,
lament the fear of my demise,
for the Sparrow did not return,
dead head of Janus did not turn,
and I am free

HUMAN RAINFALL

Pitter patter,
seas of matter
concave and turn to foam.
Chit and chatter,
ever after,
drone endless in my home.
Where is my form,
my shape and storm,
I don't know where I've been.

Now, now, child,
do not be afraid,
do not cry,
one day you'll be saved;
this dark life
shall bind you no more.

Flitter flatter,
words don't matter,
you wear a mask for all.
Slip and saunter, crying monster,
be wary of your fall.
Where is my form,
my shape and storm,
I don't know where I've been.

Try, try, child
to hold yourself up,
do not fear,
you have had enough;
this dark life
shall haunt you no more

Mutter smother,
voice of mother,
could never save me now.
Flip and falter,
will you hug her?
I am the one who drowns.
Where is my form,
my shape and storm,
I don't know where I've been.

Do not fret,
you are upside down,
sleep, sleep, child,
I say to myself;
I can save
my dark form of foam.

BROWN POWDER

I drink to her,
the red-haired girl,
with needles up her skin.

I drink to her,
I know her dark,
her demons from within.

Her eyes grew sunken,
cold and grey,
as she shrank from life with shame.

I drink to her,
the long-lost girl,
they never gave her care.

I drink to her,
for I could run
and join her if I dare.

INSOMNIA

Creeping, crawling, slimy skin
breaking bones and giving sin—
footfalls quake and shake beneath
the barren moor of troubled sleep.

The comfort gone and mind awoke,
with hellish verse she once had spoke
to make your footfalls quake and shake
in the troubled wake of troubled fate.

To Live

I claw with every teetering fingernail,
razor blades that sli-
ce and turn me to dust.
Yellowed, decaying calcium,
breathing
withthefurvorinwhichIbreathe,
withachingandclawingandexhasperation,
eyeswidewithcataractsI'm
d
  r
    o
      w
        n
          i
            n
              g
in my mental compost, in my
why's and how's and ifs and when's,
All unrealized and shouting in tandem,
unchecked voices pounding my brain to
L E T   T H E M   O U T

STOP.
The yellow fingernails against the rock-face are beginning
to crack, I look to
the bottom.
If only I were to let go, I would melt with the stones from the
beginning of time; I would no
longer be rubble but myth and legend:
a story of a golden sword, not a pile of broken, battered stone.
    l   e   t   i   t   g   o

Masochist

My fingers lace themselves on the edge of a pew
and pray to not be rid of you.
They whisper request to taste the letters of your name
that, with sweetened innocence, dance with want
as they spoil bitter in the corners of my mouth.
Your arms, may their memory cradle me,
and may the arms of another cause my body to convulse
and lead my heart to heaviness beneath their gentle touch.
My fingers dangle themselves from the quiet wood,
praying to forever sit upon that precipice,
as much in the still warm chair as the casket ahead.
Oh, and they pray to hear your calling voice from the cavern below,
so that they may spread their wings and close their eyes and know.

I beg, I beg to be possessed by the oceans of your eyes—
Father, condemn me to his love and doom me to die.
    Absolve me,
    Forgive me,
    but alas, condemn me to die.

My head falls to softened sleep on the edge of a pew,
and dreams to always know of you.
My lips ache to feel your smile behind my own
that leads these winded lungs to stop and sigh
and, distant, tugs the weary bones of my chest.

The Final Light

May the skeleton try to run,
escape the chipped wooden prison,
locked amongst mothballs and coat hangers,
and crumble upon uneven Earth
to pierce and bloody my skin
as an idol of the bruises on my heart.
The bones shall never take back their form, if I may be
    so blessed,
they will only know your fracture, and forget the rest.

I beg, I beg to suffer the torment of your sweetest smiles—
Father, condemn me to forget the peace of a child.
      Absolve me,
      Forgive me,
      but, alas, condemn me to try.

SADIST

Years from now you'll gaze out beyond,
coffee mug resting gently in your hands,
to be shattered against the tile floor
with lips turned black by years of ash.

Fridge magnets will call out my name,
squirm until formed into my memory,
for the letters there once danced along a screen
and bathe in immortality.

That's the cadence that bends your ear,
that causes a grown man to bend and weep.
Every time you touch those keys, I'll be there—
the tremble behind fingertips.

These are the lines that now fall flat,
the muse's words now read impish delight.
You'll find yourself writing—stop, and sigh,
stanza breaks alongside your mind.

Affairs of the sun pay no care;
innocent guitar shall be rid of you;
smiles and peasant skirts that bask in her light
will cause your waking eyes to bleed.

> Your heart will long for sweaty bodies, lights;
> Your heart shall miss the trespassing of fleas;
> The cat will now turn up her nose at you.

The Final Light

Or the years will feel far away,
the stench of coffee will rise from our teeth
to frame mustaches of hot chocolate—
eons woven into your arms.

Immortal letters need not pain,
the mottos may entrance your heart to laugh,
for I ache to see your sweet child's grin
that flashes briefly between ears.

That's the cadence that bends my ear,
may you wipe the tears I try to hide.
and may you brush past faded double doors
to hear arpeggios inside.

Perhaps these lines shall sing and dance,
digits itching to obey her command.
You'll find yourself writing—stop, and sigh,
under the wing of heaven's light.

Affairs of the sun will know you;
a lefty shall know your innocent touch;
"Hey There Delilah" will follow through fields—
drown in skirts and summer tinged grins.

      Your mouth will plead against the bodies, lights;
      You shall bolt to escape the siege of fleas;
      My cat will not offend but say hello.

Whether it be by kiss we say goodbye,
or a nod of the head be our reply,
call me years from now—stop, and sigh.

The Final Light

I can see you, helmet in hand, stand there,
your eyes can read the wounds of heart so bare,
call me years from now—stop, and sigh.

To her of your dreams, I extend my arm;
of joyous days I can always be part—
I shall revel in the warmth of her cheeks;
I'll rejoice in the flowers in her heart.

To you I give heed to not walk away,
for one day you shall wake up, then you'll see—
you shall find peace nuzzled within your soul,
and I pray you weep with want to show me.

4 AM

All I wanted was for lips of rose petals
to press against my own,
for my body to quake and tremble,
eyes grinning and dancing with laughter.
I know tonight they beam as pleasured pagan nymphs,
but in this dark my soul instead reverts;
the sweet kisses begin to bloody my mouth as piercing thorns;
the touches send shivers through my skin
and raise goosebumps from the dead
and hair shooting into the stagnant air.
These false idols cannot save me, for they are not you,
sweet, sweet you,
in whose arms I have never felt safer,
warmer,
enveloped by Eden's sweet embrace.

And here I am, after 4 AM—
I escape and close the door behind,
my breathing shallow, fleeting bursts.
The swallowed thorns pierce my sickened stomach walls;
the crown of spikes holds envious possession over the skin
that remembers—
the skin that longs for rose petals,
the skin that longs to be saved.

Plea for Strength

Years ago in black voids above
stars once burned and breathed their light
to converge and hum within your walls of skin
pulled tight across your aching soul.
Billions of years, lightyears through the darkness,
lost and scrambling, ashes of heaven, tumbling
and crashing again and again in and out of enlightenment,
a living, breathing cosmos, touched the Earth
as you.
Each weeping atom, each shivering divine design
formed into your weary heart
and your aching breast
and the tumult of your tears.
Your rows and chains of dust from God
did not come all this way for you to place your knees in the dirt
and pray to leave the grime behind.
You are made of stars,
billions of years converged into one single split second of time
just so you could live.
Here.
Now.

Pride

Now and again I wonder—
how many wily smiles have torn me asunder?
How many well-placed parentheses
and recycled excuses have burned me alive?

Now and again I wonder
if I will no longer stand still,
if each reverberating emotion
will finally feel free will.

Now and again I wonder—
how many times have you felt my thunder?
How many shoes and carpets meet
to tremble with my feet and downcast eyes?

Now and again I wonder
if I will no longer take the blame,
if each prideful breath of mine
will finally be torn by shame.

SOFT

If there were no wispy wind,
I would not know the currents of hot air
cascading down my back in your whispers.
If there were no guitar,
I would not know the music of your heart:
strings bring kisses before they do bruises.

I miss the caverns of your hands
that knew the softness of my arms—
without chipped wooden pencils
digging scars into crinkled pages,
how would I remember?

If there were no thin water,
I would not know the feeling of fleeting
passing through my fingers and vanishing.
If there were no winter,
I would not know the true meaning of death:
you slipped through the spaces and disappeared.

I miss the depth of your kisses
that knew the contours of my lips—
without the refreshing salve
that heals my broken, shivering skin,
how would I remember?

Without these blankets caressing
my legs concaved into my chest,
how would I remember
what it's like to be soft again?

The Constant Companion

Do not dare to deny darkness within
that permeates my aching heart to choke
pleasantries and fleeting terms of good thought.
Nay, there be no fetters along my soul,
the beast sits quiet 'fore my chamber door,
feet resting calm in front of fire warm.
The flames do not threaten to rise and bite
the curling toes that know their roaring light;
he does not leap and to the door arrive,
banging and howling as he did before.
Nay— he gives command to the bright of day,
that whispers and eddies through waking trees
to kiss Gaia's feet and bathe in the sea.
The beast's lips curl fondly forward
at the rushing sound of children's laughter,
and, polite, does not leave the door ajar.
Nay, the beast hidden is not locked away;
he warms his broken hands and sharpened nails
that glint in the touch of Hades' embrace—
by unlocked gate a suit of armor waits.

Composition

And back to the shadows we turn our gaze
to search for sunspots on our core;
we upturn heaps of soil sound
to find some carcass upon peaceful shore.

We seem to delight in this misery,
that mystery through hidden door;
Neglecting good within our hearts
that Earth makes everlasting beauty for.

OBSERVER

You wait, eyes glazed,
gazing past endless lists of countless names,
for something still to catch you there.
They flicker still,
stripping mementos of their memories
for the girl with wavy hair.

Smiles soft, profound,
curving past the cautious caricatures,
sitting solo by the sidelines.
You whisk away,
hands blistered taut and better taught with time;
you shall know the light someday.

A Letter

And when you awake, perhaps it shall be
as if Venus came from out the sea,
or as if the great giant's blood laced the grass
as newly-laden dew.
For birth resides in your veins,
and a willful ignorance has escaped
my soul in harrowed breaths
and the smell of gin
and the musk of man and nature.

When you awake, I may appear mosaic—
cracked and distant now,
with light filtering through me on Aurora's order.
All that I beg and plead, all that makes
me wring my hands with worry and distrust,
is that I do not appear vile to you—
that I will still glitter like starlight
and sparkle like the nurtured waves
even when the twilight breaks...
even when the purple haze resting calmly over the city skies
breaks.

Until then, I will clutch the cloak of darkness,
take the fabric up in my fists,
and await the defeat that always lays in wait for me.
I dread not the lonely night
but dread the coming day—
I dread the dust fluttering softly in the stagnant air;
if the words you breathed were
hello, not goodbye.

For You at 4 AM

If you happen to find your mind awake,
scrambling and restless for thoughts to take,
be eased by the chill of the night's sweet air—
for that cold comfort is everywhere.

If you happen to find your mind aware,
and not sure where or how to go from there,
return once again to gentle sleep—
and in peace your thriving soul shall keep.

Out

Every time my heart jumps to beat for you
another bit of skin flakes and falls away,
floating softly to the earth.
My knuckles more and more jab through the membrane;
pieces of my soul dissipate through the cracks
and hollows of my bones.
You are not the captain of this calcium vessel,
you are not the savior of the suffering soul—
These patches between my muscles are only mine to make,
coffee and sunshine not yours, but mine, to take,
and my choice alone to leave solemn mind.

That green dot beckons evermore,
but that beacon upon the shore shall not taunt me,
shall not spur me fast across the sea to confront its
hallowed light.
When the skies cave in I'm going to save my skin,
not yours,
and when the seas rise up and consume the land,
I will not hold fast to your side—
Your presence in mind shall not press my body to the hull,
shall not possess me to cower in my sanctuary of wood
because your feet upon the hollowed beams
sound like ours drifting in time across the open floor.
These sails are mine alone to pull or tug too tight,
my lighthouse not your dot, but my own light,
and my choice alone to be out of solemn mind.

I know this to be true, and I know myself to try—
I shall say this every day, and hope someday not to lie.

Unconventional Angel

The sky, it breathes a lullaby,
a few words of comfort to days gone by,
as red and purple descend to dark,
and poof goes out your noble spark.

I feel your arms around me still,
with words of wisdom giving me fill—
I trace us back to the start of time
to when I first began to shine.

The lake, it ripples with your grace:
a cigarette upon your shining face,
your tie-dye shirt I attempt to grasp
when I myself begin to lapse.

The sky, it breathes a lullaby;
still you and I rejoice in days gone by,
for the night is young and unafraid:
the dark is where our joys were made.

Sensus.

No Sadness Here

When your smooth thoughts descend like angels sweet
with lyres playing Apollo's steady beat,
my heart is not ravaged with empty yard:

Nay, memories are strewn across the green,
child's laughter rings as far as can be seen,
and each break and tear buds and blossoms new.

Bees of Hermes' design descend from air
to bless me with music from love affair;
no maliciousness tints the message wise.

Nay, the muses remain in draping white,
lest wond'rous journey be mistake with plight:
overturn each stone—find no sadness here.

To My Gardener

Every waking star will breathe
your name amongst the heavens,
and all the cosmos will sigh
when you join their burning ranks.

Your valor will be sung
in halls of stone,
and gods and men alike
will drink and die in your name.

You slayed no dragon,
you killed no man,
yet braved the biting breeze
of deathly, decaying wind.

You knew the frostbite
of loneliness and the fire of love,
and you tended the throbbing soul
you found buried in my chest.

Every dripping cloud will weep
when you no longer grace this earth,
and I shall lie beside your stone
and watch you will the grass to grow.

SILENT

No words, no words my gentle soul,
take your tongue from 'tween your teeth
and let it rest calmly in your mouth.
       I know what you mean to say.

Simply read my eyes and smile soft;
you need no excuse for your bashful lips—
you may release the pressure from your aching lungs.

Hush now, be not concerned
with the way I bite my lip and grin at you—
hold fast to the way you intend to be.

No words, no words, my child in bronze,
I do not demand you remove your armor
and let your shield clatter to the floor.
       I know what you mean to say.

Just nod and then I will know your mind;
speak through the beating in your chest
and then you may know mine.

I have always known the words you mean to say;
you have always known the words I mean to say.

Ecstasy

Away, away
go cares with flicks of wrists
and the swishes of woven skirts and curls
that smell of sweat and starlight.
Away go the worries that boil and wart
in concave lines that stress the skin.
A million beads of sun fill rooms,
fill eyes,
fill the souls of nonbelievers as the floor gives way and they
begin to fly—
And silence,
a deafness,
hangs around the moment in time,
a breath of smoke catching in your neighbor's mouth.
Breathe the coolness and the heat,
the fog of ancestral passes and the release of carefree children
on their journey far beyond.
Breathe the frigid night and release the day
from your soul.
Away, away
go the cares,
and away is night burned by the light.

Woodwork Watcher

I am a part of the woodwork on the wall.
I am the creaking and groaning of old
beams and little niches of half-broken
nails and stains of blue cheese.

I am the writing on the whiteboard, day in, day out,
as the calendar runs its course and my
charges run their hearts through and through
with the glory of youth.

I am the watcher on the wall,
and my skin will seep into the grain,
a constant, a witness of love and loss
and rebirth.

Long after I go, here I shall remain,
a reminder to live for those hands
pressed against the wall.

Missing Piece

Hail, hark—
A flutter passes over the horizon,
a drifting blue across the terrain
of midsummer crimson.
And do I smell lilacs in the air?
Do I see the tenacity of African violets
turning parched lips from the dancing rain
and grasses tipped with frosted caps
bearing themselves, their brothers, their sisters?

I can taste toes in the water
and feel vanilla melting upon the tongue;
I can breathe the currents of the air.

I can taste your blushes and
feel your shadow and
breathe your air.

Innocent Peace

It is as if love has never left us—
as if every ring of joy has festered in our unburdened souls
since we were conceived,
and the pangs of despair avoided us.
For the sweet caress of your arms
wrapped around my folded soul is so innocent,
so untainted by the foul pain of what we have seen,
that it seems impossible for darkness to have even breathed
within its proximity,
or for death to have brushed its rightness.
Is this why my body quakes when I am not with you?
Because you are a flaming ethereal star,
and without your shelter every breeze is cold and insulting
and every breath heavy?
Your absence bites frosty on my frozen lips,
and your hands fit snugly into my soul.

Greek Pairs

I love to watch pairs—
in love, in friendship,
the way their hair falls tells all.

People in love seem to stand alone:
reliefs against a painted street
with small figurines marching along
a road paved with moonlight.

People in friendship, such a powerful force,
appear to be everywhere at once.
Everything that occurs around them
purposeful, as a guided tour of reality,
simultaneously as removed as alive.
                A musician approaches,
                  flowers in hand,
                skin caked with dirt and
              hands bound by cloth—
He is the epitome of the divine;
he tells us we are beautiful.

I smile at them,
absorbed in their own existence,
grinning into each other—
waterfalls fumbling over one another's rocky grooves.
    They are the epitome of the divine;
    I tell them they are beautiful.

Odysseus

Go then, if you must,
across the foaming sea to lands beyond,
but forget not my heart of trust
that lies peacefully in your hands.

I will not fret, nor
call in fear; walk head high and shoulders broad—
do not forget to glance before
you never see my eyes again.

Do not despair, but
find your pride; take on your journey with joy.
If your heart be woefully shut,
go back, look fondly on my love.

Go then, if you must,
trust your trembling boots to a quest unsure.
Remember I was more than lust,
and I loved your waking dreams.

An Ode to Sunlight

Mind not where the droplets of water fall
as they descend in pillars of light and dust
to caverns below and land at the feet
of those paralyzed in awe of glory through the trees.

May you remain transfixed on the scurrying
of little friends darting up pillars and beneath the leaves,
and the leaves blowing slowly above
to fall asleep quietly in your hands.

The rushing currents, a dragon's tail
that whisks back and forth in the warm embrace
of the sun of midafternoon, is easy
to run your fingers along and believe in something to.

See how fleeting the water be,
yet how persistent, how meaningful
each little child of current is as it leaps and bounds
down nature's earthen steps.

Whether it collects in pools, stagnant, staring,
or runs its course to dissipate into the earth
and never flow again, or whether
it shall create beauties of caverns that glisten in twilight,

mind not where the droplets of water fall.
Pray you see them in the heavens' glare;
pray you run your hand along flanks of moss,
and pray you catch those leaves again.

Bystander

Why do I fear?
There is glistening on the lake—
I tremble, I glance from the corner of my eye,
awaiting siege on my small golden throne.
You pay me no mind.

But your language is unknown to me,
and you are too close for comfort:
the calls resemble battle cries.
I brace myself and look away…
A shout, a cry! Wings soar past
my head, buffeting my hair
with *Notos'* mighty hand.

I close my eyes—
I can no longer see the lake,
the gentle trees kissing their reflections,
white petals on the shoreline pushing
through the darkening of fall.

And then… release.

Alas, you meant me no harm;
I am merely a carving on the water's edge,
a tiny piece of lawn—
Thus you bathe in the richness of the sun,
and I, too, am once again allowed peace of mind.

I stifle public laughter in my chest
and smile fondly across the way
to the clouds crested with shine
and the willows dancing in delight.

        I wonder—
                why was I ever afraid?

OTHER

I have never been alone.
Fairies of the wood oft come to bid me follow,
with legs of silken sunlight winking from billowing dresses
and braided hair framing their lovely faces.
Their hands are smooth as ladies fair,
yet their eyes are possessed by endless time:
a jovial wisdom peeks between their grinning lips.

Oft they send sweet songs upon my ears,
meandering past forests broad and highways long,
keeping my head forward and my eyes bright
against any scourge of winter that bites my heart.

They have wings of pale silver, eyes of swift horizons,
and they follow me as Pan in party grand
to dance and whistle and caress my hair.
They lay beneath wise old trees and kiss the flowers sweet
and run their fingers through burnt fields of my despair,
sending blades of grass into vibrant green—
tiny arms outstretched, rejoice in newfound meaning.

I have never been alone.
When my heart feels forbidden from the gates of peace,
and my hands feel pale at Heaven's door,
the Fairies chisel at my feet glued,
and seek to take me there once more.

Absent Touch

Your laughter no longer brings my heart to pain;
my sweet sorrow exists ever stiller in my chest,
tranquil in the knowledge that you love me.

Your voice no longer rings futile drums of war;
my gentle hands feel safe with the memory of yours,
peaceful in the knowledge that you love me.

I do not require that you love me by my side,
but tender in my heart I know, and tender there reside.

Home is Where the Heart is

Everyday you'll be home to me.
When I come back in the chill of night,
and the call of frogs slips softly past my steady ears,
and the wind tickles my chin and dampens my eyes,
I will be at home in your memory.
When I awake by the beating light of morn,
and the red tints the edges of clouds so white,
dancing through the sky, arms entwined,
and souls locked in waltz upon the chem trails,
I will come home to you.
And your whispers will kiss my frozen toes
snuggled beneath rustling blankets,
and your kindness will lay my restless head to rest.
Your dreams shall bring me to dream;
your steps I will follow across sea and terrain,
and then I will come home to you.
Every night I drift to easy sleep
my eyes will flutter beneath canopies of blinking stars,
and I will come home to you in my heart.

LOSE MY VOICE

Take from my lips these words, O gentle light,
and make a space for Heaven's calm respite.
The tongue that wag doth often stay
by the rotting pier of mind's decay.

Grip my soul and be my muse,
'tween decisions rough, I'll ne'er choose.
Find for me a place of calm
where water runneth over gentle palm.

Take from my lips these words, O gentle night,
and in silent absence discover might,
For those who teach must first not say,
and need understand the wise old day.

New Year's Eve

Loved be the peaceful soul that peaceful sits
with champagne drying apologetically on the backs of hands
that had flown feverishly into the air at the drop of a shimmering ball
and flung aside to make way for joining lips and laughing eyes
to revel in secrets and long-lost loves.

I may kiss a picture frame
and hold bits of paper to my chest.
My feet may decide to step in time
to blonde hair rushed into a bun, parted from the eyes,
to better conduct a rejoicing song
that reeks of dry wine and sweet perfume
and memories of childhood glee
that bob in time to the banging of plastic beads
and the tearing of flimsy paper crowns.

Let me blow a candle out for you,
and you hours behind know the wishes from future sent;
reach your timid fingers up by your head
and the wind will hold them there.

Let the Light In

Let not rage tempt thy noble heart
and make ye quick to shake with roaring thunder
or tremble with the darkness of that foreboding cloud.
Let air go peaceful through your painful lungs,
and may ye permit that breeze pass in steady time.
May your limbs rest easy and breathe;
may the lavender in your soul kiss your ears,
and may you close your weary eyes
and press your brow to Vesta's chest.
Shh, lay your worried calm beside the battle lines,
allow your words to be led by Eirene's hand—
Turn your eyes toward Minerva bright
when Ares' fire tries to blind your sight.

Elegy

What a time to die by friends such as these;
our banners bill'wing break the open air,
and we by way of sword our freedom seize,
or with pride leave our broken bodies there.

How honorable to by valk'rie lie;
how well to your glory your armor fits,
and by way of wing take to open sky
where on golden throne waiting Odin sits.

May peaceful slumber shade the weary we,
for in forever song our valor be.

LAST DANCE

Let me dance on your toes again,
one day when lights are low and music deep,
with twinkling stars peeping and giggling at the windowsill,
and our breaths lacking the familiar tint of tequila,
just present.
Let those toes tremble with cold,
one night when the leaves have come and gone,
with pajama pant legs rolled up to come not between,
and our eyes lacking the familiar ferocity of want,
just slow.
Let there be a gaze waiting above,
one time when I lift my face from watching steps
with laughter stumbling breathlessly over our chins and fingers,
and our skin lacking the familiar tremble of unknown desire,
just simple.
And we shall slow dance, with no need for counts of three—
our feet will glide effortlessly over once barren ground;
flowers will grow where seeds in tear capsules fall free,
and your memory will rest in my breast safe and sound.

I Found You

I have been looking for you.
I never before knew what compelled my eyes
to gaze and linger in distorted passing glass—
perhaps there was a narcissism in my bending face,
perhaps there were stories drifting in the trails
of the passerby.
In everyone I have ever loved,
I have been looking for you.
There has always been something,
a deep tremble in my belly,
a twitch in my fingers,
a rise in the hair on the back of my neck
(lifting to tickle my timid skin),
as I scanned the chasms of their eyes.
There has always been something in their jawline,
the texture of simple waves and prickly beards.
I have been looking for you—
it has never been the garb of the wearer,
but the one who wears it.
Their coats always hung from them too loosely,
their smiles always too hard-pressed 'tween their teeth,
voices airy or deep, gracing Heaven's clouds too soon
or Hell's breadth too far.
I have touched hand to cheek far too many times,
my eyes have darted not as adventurers, but couriers—
"Take me to the owner of this heart," I say,
"I wish to speak to your Lord here."

The Final Light

I have scanned my own globes,
seeking, praying, dreaming of some unknown knowl-
 edge on high
to grace my waking mind.
But here you are.
Alas, here you are,
and message in hand, stirrups straight, I ride home,
and I know I have not been searching for what,
but for whom.

Earning a Lover's Wings

I witness purple tendrils take
your eyes away from mine and to the wings
that spread and engulf our souls high
above the toils earthly bodies make.

Hands, scattered, glowing rays,
extend to tear my skin from off my bones,
and fear departs from waking heart,
and we gaze upon where our body lays.

Ecstasy drips from our Lord's palm,
sticky scarlet that seeps into the Earth.
My lips yearned to suckle from the ground,
and in that urgency our mouth found calm.

Only in your arms do I learn;
our rotations we no more make;
to the stars fixed we do return
and know the message that was spake.

Specter

Let me be a shimmering force that hangs beside your bedframe;
my wispy fingers will pass through your hair of silk,
and my tears will be sweet shades of dew upon your resting cheeks.

Let me never know the sensitive fingertips that once felt your brow,
or once brushed lightly upon your relaxing arm—
Allow my feet to dangle from the mattress and mix with the air;
allow you to look deep into my heart and know not that I am there.

I need not more than to be inches from your soul,
which grows closer as our bodies move away—
I need not more than my violet form
to give sentience to your waking shadow.

This is all I ask the lord of light:
to turn me to transcendent specks of dust
so I may filter through your window bars
and as a specter, cradle you.

IF IS THE SEA

If is the Sea—
the mysteries of life
hidden beneath the waves.

A darkness fades;
translucent water waves
at the sight of light.

It is unknown;
the tide may rise one day,
fall the following night.

If is the Sea—
she shall repay the sand
to wait at her feet.

Or tide shall lie;
sun betrays dark beneath
so trust I do not know.

Implore pain take
refuge in aching soul—
move that pain to grow.

TENANTS

A knock—
heavy, hollow, clear,
to let myself inside.

Rain falls
heavy, hollow, clear,
and I wait politely.

A man calls, his voice
heavy, hollow, clear,
and he comes to meet me.

"This house is
heavy, hollow, clear,
and no one has lived here
in quite some time."

The man enters the house,
eerie, cold, ill,
and extends his hand for me.

The sound of droplets,
eerie, cold, ill,
pitter on the window panes.

A thump—
eerie, cold, ill,
upon the cellar door.

The Final Light

"This house is
eerie, cold, ill;
do not pay heed
to the pains of this place."

A touch—
calm, sweet, quiet,
graces my arm.

Tears upon my shoulder,
calm, sweet, quiet;
a presence holds me.

The man holds me,
calm, sweet, quiet,
until my shaking stops.

"This house is
calm, sweet, quiet,
the ghosts here have care;
do not fear them."

The man eyes me,
warm, knowing, kind,
and leads me to a garden.
A fountain runs,
warm, knowing, kind,
enveloped by light.

A silence—
warm, knowing, kind,
as I let myself outside.

The Final Light

"This place is
warm, knowing, kind;
drink from the pool
and the house shall not feel lonely."

A drink—
heavy, hollow, clear,
permeates my soul.

The rain sprinkles,
heavy, hollow, clear,
born from a cloudless sky.

I call to a man,
heavy, hollow, clear,
waiting at the door.

"This house appears
heavy, hollow, clear,
but it is filled with tenants
peaceful, loving, whole."

I enter the house,
peaceful, loving, whole,
and extend my hand to him.

My Moonlight

Tread softly, my little moon;
you have a heart of gold and arrows on your back—
do not be so afraid to come into the day,
when the trees are asleep and the animals away.

Hark to the sound of birds
as they break away into the morning sun—
bend down to test the soil slipping through
your fingers tinged with midsummer dew.

I know you to be fierce
and filled with a pride worthy of the gods,
but you often must dispel that seed of doubt
that warns of ambient evils you know not about.

Tread firmly, my courageous moon,
you know not the power of your glistening soul—
do not be so afraid to trust the world's love,
and assign your fate to something higher above.

MIRACLE

Grip tight my hand and take me to the sea,
if there sweet peace amongst the algae be,
and guide my hand along the rising tide,
so I may see ebb and flow coincide.

Let my timid fingers touch rocks of braille;
may noise be 'nough to fasten tow'ring sail.
Tie my body fast to post, drift along,
with lyre join with lovely siren song.

Draw out great theories out across the sand,
so I may fear the water as little as I land.
May your rocky hands part the blue for me,
and by way of miracles teach the blind to see.